A Note to Parents

Eyewitness Readers is a compelling new program
for beginning readers, designed in conjunction with
leading literacy experts, including Dr. Linda Gambrell,
President of the National Reading Conference and past
board member of the International Reading Association.

Eyewitness has become the most trusted name in
illustrated books, and this new series combines the highly
visual *Eyewitness* approach with engaging, easy-to-read
stories. Each *Eyewitness Reader* is guaranteed to
capture a child's interest while developing his or her
reading skills, general knowledge, and love of reading.

The four levels of *Eyewitness Readers* are aimed
at different reading abilities, enabling you to choose
the books that are exactly right for your children:

Level 1, for **Preschool to Grade 1**
Level 2, for **Grades 1 to 3**
Level 3, for **Grades 2 and 3**
Level 4, for **Grades 2 to 4**

The "normal" age at which a child begins to read
can be anywhere from three to eight years old, so these
levels are intended only as a general guideline.

No matter which level you select, you can be sure
that you are helping your child learn to read, then
read to learn!

A DK PUBLISHING BOOK
www.dk.com

Created by Leapfrog Press Ltd

Project Editor Elizabeth Bacon
Art Editor Rebecca Johns

For Dorling Kindersley
Senior Editor Mary Atkinson
Managing Art Editor Peter Bailey
Production Melanie Dowland
Picture Researcher Jo Walton
Jacket design Chris Drew
U. S. Editor Regina Kahney

Reading Consultant
Linda B. Gambrell, Ph.D.

First American Edition, 1999
4 6 8 10 9 7 5
Published in the United States by DK Publishing, Inc.
95 Madison Avenue, New York, New York 10016

Published in Great Britain by Dorling Kindersley Limited.

Eyewitness Readers™ is a trademark of Dorling Kindersley Limited, London.

Library of Congress Cataloging-in-Publication Data

Donkin, Andrew.
    Going for Gold / by Andrew Donkin. — 1st American ed.
      p.   cm. — (Eyewitness readers)
    Summary: Profiles notable Olympic athletes who overcame the odds
to win gold medals, including Jesse Owens, Shelley Mann, and Kerri
Strug.
    ISBN 0-7894-4765-7. — ISBN 0-7894-4764-9 (pbk.)
    1. Athletes Biography Juvenile literature. 2. Olympics Juvenile
literature. [1. Athletes. 2. Olympics—History.] I. Title.
II. Series.
GV697.A1D65   1999
796'.092'2—dc21
[B]
                                                    99-26070
                                                        CIP

Color reproduction by Colourscan, Singapore
Printed and bound in Belgium by Proost

The publisher would like to thank the following
for their kind permission to reproduce their photographs:
Key: t=top, a=above, b=below, l=left, r=right, c=centre

Action Plus: 14b; AKG London Ltd: 6b;
Allsport: 2, 4bl, 6t, 7t, 10t, 13, 20t, 37, 43b, 44t, 44–5b;
Associated Sports Photography: 21b, 25; Corbis UK Ltd: 8b;
DK Picture Library/National Maritime Museum: 12b;
/Robert Opie: 21t; Empics: 36b; Hulton Getty: 10b, 23;
Impact Photos/Jorn Stjerneklar: 22b;
Popperfoto: 5br, 14t, 15b, 36t, 39, 40, 42, 45t; Rex Features: 15t;
Science Photo Library 24b; Sporting Pictures: 4tl;
Supersport/Eileen Langsley: 38t, 40t;
Topham Picturepoint: 7b, 9, 11, 24t, 43t

Additional photography by Philip Dowell, John Garrett, Dave King, David Spence

Contents

EYEWITNESS READERS

Level **4**

GRADES 2-4

GOING FOR GOLD!

Written by Andrew Donkin

DK PUBLISHING, INC.

Olympic flag
The Olympic symbol's five rings stand for Europe, Asia, Africa, Australia, and America.

Jesse Owens
This athlete's performance at the 1936 Games remains an inspiration to young athletes worldwide.

Let the Games begin!

Once every four years, the greatest athletes in the world gather together in one city to take part in the biggest sporting event on earth – the summer Olympic Games.

Winning a gold medal is the ultimate aim of every competitor in each of the many events. Athletes spend long and often lonely years training hard for the great Games.

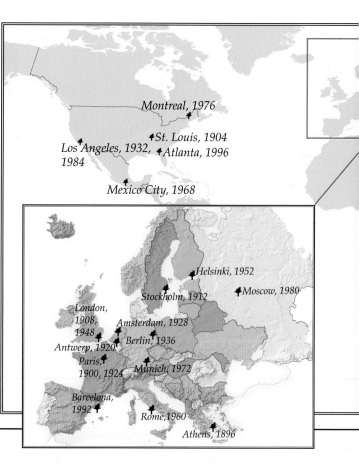

Montreal, 1976

St. Louis, 1904
Los Angeles, 1932, Atlanta, 1996
1984

Mexico City, 1968

Helsinki, 1952
Stockholm, 1912
Moscow, 1980
London, 1908, 1948
Amsterdam, 1928
Antwerp, 1920
Berlin, 1936
Paris, 1900, 1924
Munich, 1972
Barcelona, 1992
Rome, 1960
Athens, 1896

After all that work, the athletes spend only a few hours at the Olympic Games competing against the "best of the best."

In this book you'll meet some of the greatest Olympians of all time. Each one had to overcome incredible obstacles on their way to a gold medal.

But first, how did the Olympic Games begin?

The flame
The Olympic motto is "Swifter, higher, stronger."
The torch flame symbolizes this motto.

Seoul, 1988 *Tokyo, 1964*

Sydney, 2000
Melbourne, 1956

Kerri Strug
Gymnast Kerri Strug faced an agonizing challenge in the 1996 Atlanta Games.

5

The ancient Games

The first recorded Olympic Games took place in the small Greek city of Olympia nearly 3,000 years ago, in 776 BC.

These games consisted of just a single sprint race. As word of the games spread, more people wanted to take part. The organizers soon added other events, such as long-distance races, throwing, wrestling, and chariot racing.

Back track
The earliest Olympians raced on a track that was 629 ft (192 meters) long.

This illustration from a Greek vase, from 400 BC, shows two Olympic wrestlers.

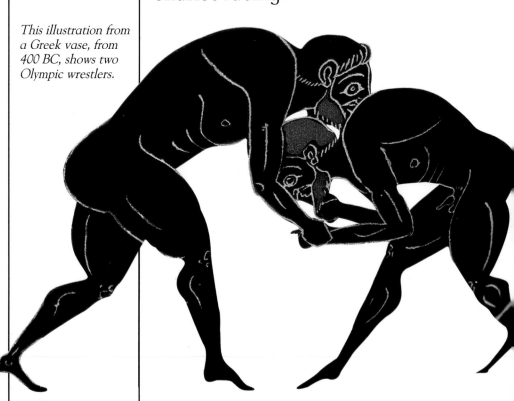

A Greek king ordered that a magnificent stone stadium be built so that a crowd of thousands could watch the sporting drama unfold.

Women were forbidden to attend the Games. If a woman spectator was discovered, she was hurled off a nearby cliff.

The ancient Games were held every four years until a Roman emperor banned them in AD 393. The stadium gradually fell into ruin.

Centuries later, in 1829, the ruins were discovered by French archeologists (ar-key-OL-oh-jists). An Olympic enthusiast, Baron Pierre de Coubertin (coo-ber-TAN), organized the first modern Olympics. The Games were held in Greece in 1896.

Practice ground
Archeologists also uncovered the remains of the Olympians' training area, called the Palaestra (pal-AYE-strah).

Fresh start
The first event of the 1896 Olympic Games was an 100-meter sprint. Thomas Burke of the U.S. won the race in 12 seconds.

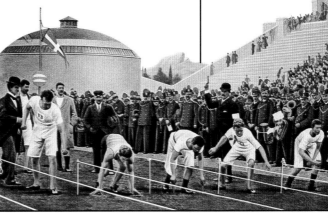

Good timing
Coach Riley's stopwatch could measure Jesse's speed to a tenth of a second. Modern stopwatches can measure a hundredth of a second.

Rising star
This 1933 photo shows Jesse winning a 200-meter (220-yard) dash in an interschools competition.

The greatest

"Faster!" shouted Coach Riley, looking down at his stopwatch as Jesse Owens hurtled past him. Jesse took giant strides, moving powerfully around the running track.

Coach Riley was Jesse's trainer at high school in Ohio, which Jesse attended in the early 1930s.

Riley had never seen anyone with such natural athletic talent as Jesse, but his physical and mental skills needed to be developed.

Riley taught Jesse special techniques to help him get the best sprint start and to run with a smoother, quicker motion:

"Keep your head and body low and pump your arms hard, Jesse," said Riley.

"Now bounce off that track. Run like the ground is on fire!" he shouted to Jesse.

Times were hard for many Americans. At home, Jesse's family struggled to make ends meet. Sometimes they didn't even have enough money for firewood. After school and on the weekends, Jesse delivered groceries in the neighborhood to earn a little extra money for his family.

This meant that his hour-long training sessions had to take place early in the morning, before school started.

Jesse learned fast and worked hard. His dedication paid off. In high school he entered 79 races and won an amazing 75 of them!

Team spirit
Jesse Owens with his American teammates. In all, the U.S. team took home 56 medals, 24 of which were gold!

In 1936, Jesse was thrilled to be chosen as part of the American team for the Berlin Olympic Games in Germany. Jesse was entered in three track events: the 100 meters, the 200 meters, and the long jump.

The Games took place in a huge new stadium. The Olympic torch was lit on Mount Olympus in Greece.

It was carried to Berlin by a series of runners. A crowd of 100,000 people cheered as the last runner carried the Olympic torch into the stadium.

Among the spectators was Adolf Hitler, the leader of Germany. Hitler was hoping that athletes from his beloved home country would show the world their physical superiority. Could Jesse Owens steal a gold medal from under Hitler's nose?

Six runners lined up for the final of the 100 meters.

"Around me are five of the fastest human beings on the planet, and they all want to beat me to the finish line," Jesse thought. "After all the training I've done since high school, everything rests on the next ten seconds."

Then he focused his mind on the track ahead.

The leader
Hitler wanted to impress the world by staging one of the most spectacular Olympics ever. The event was broadcast on screens in 25 Berlin theaters.

11

Ready, set...
Gunshots are still used to start Olympic sprint races. Today, sprinters push off from starting blocks, which can detect false starts within 0.1 seconds.

In many Olympic events, an official shows a red flag when a foul has taken place.

"Bang!"

The starter fired his gun and the six finalists burst away from the "scratch" line. Jesse got a great start and began running smoothly. After just a few strides, he began to pull away from the pack, his faster running style eating up the ground in front of him.

Jesse blasted through the finish line in 10.3 seconds – a time equal to the world record! Jesse had won his first gold medal.

The next day, Jesse returned to the stadium and ran into trouble. He was competing in the long jump, and had to do three jumps in his attempt to qualify for the final.

"Foul jump!" shouted the official, raising a red flag. For the second time Jesse's foot had gone over the edge of the takeoff board. If he fouled again, he'd be disqualified.

Jesse calmly retraced his steps back from the takeoff board, then turned and started the run up for his final jump. Jesse took off cleanly and sailed through the air.

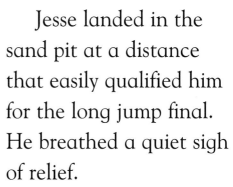

Friendly rivals
Luz Long befriended Jesse in full view of Hitler and his supporters, who held strongly racist beliefs.

Baton buddy
There are four runners in an Olympic relay team. Each sprints an 100-meter "leg" of the race, then passes a baton to the next runner. The fastest runner in the team runs the last 100 meters.

Jesse landed in the sand pit at a distance that easily qualified him for the long jump final. He breathed a quiet sigh of relief.

In the final, Jesse came head to head with his German rival, Luz Long. It was Long who had to settle for the silver when Jesse set a new Olympic record with a jump of 8.06 meters (26 ft).

Two days later, Jesse won gold in the 200 meters with a time of 20.7 seconds, knocking a full half second off the previous best Olympic time. Jesse thought that his third gold medal would be his last, but a surprise was in store.

"We want you to run the last leg of the relay race," explained the manager of the American team. He thought that with Jesse on the team, it couldn't lose. He was right.

The Americans triumphed. They finished 1.33 seconds ahead of the German team.

A sportswriter described Jesse's run as being "as smooth as the west wind" – a fitting tribute to one of the greatest Olympians of all time.

Gold medal
To win an Olympic gold medal is every competitor's dream. U. S. swimmer Mark Spitz won seven gold medals in 1972. No one has yet broken his great record.

Berlin 1936
Very high standards were set at the 1936 Games. There were numerous world-record breakers. Owen's 26-foot long jump record remained unbeaten for 25 years!

15

In the swim of it

Some athletes have far greater challenges to face than beating their rivals on their way to success at the Olympics. To earn her medal, American Shelley Mann had to overcome a terrible disease that almost paralyzed her whole body.

In 1945, the doctors looking after six-year-old Shelley recognized the classic signs of polio. They told her parents that Shelley's case was severe. She could hardly move.

Healing waters
Many doctors recommend exercises in warm water to treat muscular illnesses.

Polio
Polio is a disease that affects part of the spinal cord and causes paralysis. All children should be vaccinated against polio.

At the age of ten, Shelley's family took her swimming at a summer camp in Maryland. She couldn't play golf or tennis with the other children, but she could mix with them in the pool.

Floating weightless in the warm water, Shelley began to move her weakened limbs.

"Lift your arms, Shelley. You can do it," her mother encouraged her.

Every day in the pool, Shelley worked to get the strength back in her body. It was difficult work, but swimming soon became the most important thing in her life.

By the age of twelve, Shelley had begun competitive training in Washington, D.C. She was a natural at every stroke she tried.

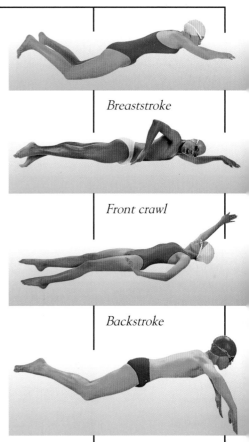

Breaststroke

Front crawl

Backstroke

Butterfly

Racing strokes
When Shelley was training, the breaststroke became the fourth stroke swum in competitions. Shelley swam medleys, where a swimmer does two lengths of each of the four strokes.

Dawn Fraser
Australia's Dawn Fraser swam in Sydney Harbor five hours a day to train for the Melbourne Olympics. She set the 100-meter freestyle record.

Butterfly
A swimmer doing butterfly makes butterfly shapes in the water. He or she uses a strong, double-arm pull and an up and down "dolphin kick" with his or her legs.

Shelley swam for an hour or more every day before and after school.

"I love to swim, and I love to win, so I work hard without knowing it," she said.

In the early 1950s, Shelley won the U.S. National Championship for butterfly, backstroke, freestyle, and medley races and was part of a record-breaking relay team. At the age of 17, Shelley found herself selected for the 1956 Olympic Games in Melbourne, Australia.

"You have to have the desire and you have to practice. Those are the two most important things," she said, just before the Games began.

She didn't begin well, placing sixth in the 100-meter freestyle.

In the 100-meter butterfly, Shelley stood waiting for the starter's signal. As the sound echoed around the pool, Shelley dived into the water, her powerful butterfly stroke propelling her down the pool. She touched home in a time of 1 minute 11 seconds, a new Olympic record.

As Shelley received her medal, tears ran down her face. Her hard work and willpower had paid off. The girl who couldn't move a muscle had struck gold.

Celebrity
After her Olympic win, Shelley Mann became a celebrity. She traveled the world, meeting thousands of officials. But her heart was with her friends and family. Her favorite place was "in a nice, warm bed with a cup of hot chocolate."

Shelley is wearing the official uniform of the U.S. Olympic team at the 1956 Olympics.

Never give up

Mamo Wolde pushed forward with his aching legs and forced himself to take another stride along the running track.

Mamo was on his last lap of the 10,000 meters at the 1964 Tokyo Games. More than anything else, he wanted to take home an Olympic medal.

He looked ahead and fixed his eyes on the three runners in front of him. Using every last ounce of strength, Mamo increased his speed and began gaining on the men ahead. However, as the three runners in front of him approached the finish line, they too increased their pace.

Mamo could only watch as others won the gold, silver, and bronze medals.

He came in fourth place and was bitterly disappointed.

Get a grip!
Runners wear spiked shoes on an Olympic stadium track. Spikes provide a good grip on the rubber or plastic surface. Marathon runners don't use spikes, as they run on hard roads.

Spiked shoes

Long-distance shoes

Mamo walked over to the winner, American William Mills, and congratulated him.

This was not Mamo's first defeat at the Olympics. At the 1956 Melbourne Games in Australia, he had come last in the 10,000 meters. Now in the Tokyo stadium, Mamo watched Mills get his gold medal.

"I am not finished yet," Mamo told himself. "I'll be back and going for gold in four years' time."

TV winners
TV became popular in the late 1950s. In 1964, millions watched the Tokyo Games on their sets.

Pasta

Potato

Peanuts

Athletes' diet
Top athletes
like Mamo eat
a simple diet
to maintain
fitness. They
eat starchy
foods, like those
shown above.

*The high plains of
Ethiopia, where
Mamo trained
with Abebe.*

Mamo returned to his native
Ethiopia in Africa and back to
his job as a member of the
Ethiopian Imperial Bodyguard.

Every day, Mamo went on
a training run many miles across
the rough, barren mountains.

Mamo's friend, Abebe Bikila,
often joined him.

Abebe's Olympic career had
been very different from Mamo's.
Abebe had won the gold medal for
the 26-mile marathon at the last
two Olympic Games. Abebe decided
to give his good friend some advice.

One hot, dry evening the two men were jogging through the fading rays of an African sunset.

"Maybe the races you're running are too short for you," suggested Abebe. "Your spirit wants to keep running. You should let it," he suggested.

"But I tried a marathon once before and didn't even finish it," responded Mamo.

"So, try again until you do. One thing I've learned is never give up," said Abebe, before sprinting ahead. His simple words took root in Mamo's mind.

23

High and dry
Mexico City is 2,300 meters (7,500 ft) above sea-level. Some athletes at the 1968 Games, such as Mamo, were used to heights. Others suffered from altitude (height) sickness.

Marathon man
In 490 BC a messenger ran 24 miles (38 kilometers) to report a Greek victory at the Battle of Marathon. This run inspired the first marathon race.

Inspired by Abebe, Mamo made sure of his place in the starting line for the 1968 marathon in Mexico City.

Abebe Bikila was defending his title and was favored to win. Mamo, however, had other ideas. He had planned his tactics.

As the race started, Mamo let some of the better-known athletes set the pace, but made sure that he was not far behind them.

About halfway through the 26-mile (41.6-kilometer) race, Mamo broke away from the rest and opened up a good lead. Abebe retired with a leg injury.

Mamo powered on. No matter how his legs ached, no matter how hot and thirsty he was, uphill and down, he carried on for mile after mile.

A modern marathon runner stops for a drink.

His willpower paid off and he entered the stadium to wild cheers. He was so far ahead that by the time the second runner had reached the stadium, Mamo had run round it in a "lap of honor" to celebrate his victory.

Mamo knew for sure that going for gold meant never giving up.

Big cheat
The first man into the stadium in the 1904 marathon was Fred Lorz. But he had accepted a lift for 11 miles (18 kilometers) of the race!

25

Decathlon
Four of the decathlon events are track events: 100 meters, 400 meters, 1,500 meters, 110-meter hurdles. The other six are field events: the long jump, high jump, shot put, discus, javelin, and pole vault.

The rivals

Daley Thompson wiped the sweat from his forehead. He stared up at the scoreboard, waiting for his winning time in the 100-meter sprint, the first event in the 1984 Los Angeles Olympics decathlon.

Decathletes are ultimate sportsmen and women. They compete in a grueling two-day series of ten track and field events. They score points for their performance in each event – the athlete with the most points wins.

Ball used for the shot put

The athlete throws the javelin as far as he can.

Only one hand may be used to throw the shot put. It must be in front of the shoulders.

Thompson had won the decathlon gold medal in Moscow in 1980. He was determined to write himself into history as the second man to win two decathlon golds.

Thompson's 100-meter time of 10.44 seconds flashed up on the board. He waved to the crowd, knowing how much his fans enjoyed watching him. He also knew that to win the competition he'd have to give the performance of a lifetime. He had an arch-rival, and it was showdown time.

Moscow 1980
Every Olympic Games has a mascot. The first was a red jaguar for the 1968 Mexico Games. The mascot for the 1980 Moscow Games was Misha the Bear.

The athlete prepares to throw the wood and metal discus.

Athletes must leap 10 hurdles in any hurdle race. They are not disqualified for knocking down a hurdle.

L.A. style
The opening
ceremony of the
1984 Games
was amazing,
with marching
bands and a
display of flags
from nations
taking part.

Rival runners
British runners
Steve Ovett
and Sebastian
Coe competed
fiercely in 1980
and 1984. Coe
eventually won
more medals.

Jurgen Hingsen was a huge, powerfully built West German decathlete. He had stolen the decathlon world record from Thompson twice.

Before Thompson had arrived at the Los Angeles Games, newspaper reporters had asked him if he felt threatened by Hingsen.

"There's only one way Hingsen's going to take a gold medal home. He'll have to steal mine," Thompson replied.

Hingsen had come third in the 100 meters and Thompson also beat him in the long jump. But the battle had only just begun; Hingsen began to fight back. He did better in the shot put than Thompson, and won the high jump competition with a jump of 2.12 meters (7 ft).

The punishing duel continued on the morning of the second day, when the crowd watched a thrilling 110-meter hurdle race. The two athletes hurtled neck and neck down the track. Thompson's fans rose to their feet to see Hingsen beat him by just 0.04 seconds.

Outstanding
Other great performances in the 1984 L.A. Games included those by American sprinter Carl Lewis, who equalled Jesse Owens' feat of winning four gold medals on the track.

Hingsen had previously beaten Thompson by a whisker in the hurdle race of the 1983 Helsinki World Athletics Championships.

Discus
The discus dates back to the eighth century BC. The modern discus is made of wood with a metal rim.

Discus throw
The athlete releases the discus after turning.
The throw takes place from inside a cage to avoid accidents.

Thompson was now in the lead, but only by a few points.

The moment that decided the great battle came in the discus competition. Thompson fouled his first two throws, while Hingsen achieved a huge distance of 50.82 meters (166.68 ft).

If Thompson fouled his last throw, his rival would take the lead.

Thompson thrived under the pressure. He knew that his fans were on the edge of their seats, wondering what he would do next. He picked up the discus and lined himself up in the throwing circle, concentrating hard. Then, with all his strength, he spun around and propelled the discus far into the air. It was a clean throw. He scored a distance of 46.56 meters (152.7 ft), not enough to beat Hingsen, but enough to keep his overall lead.

After that, Thompson could do no wrong. He beat Hingsen in the pole vault and the javelin, although Hingsen did better in the 1,500 meters, ensuring a silver medal for him. Thompson hadn't beaten Hingsen's world record, but he didn't care – he'd won the gold.

"People don't remember world records," he said. "They remember Olympic champions – like me!"

Pole vault
In this event, the athlete pushes off from the ground, bends the pole with his weight, and levers himself over the bar.

Superstar
Jurgen Hingsen said of his rival: "Daley is truly the greatest among us, for he has no weaknesses."

31

Game, set, and match

Spanish village
The city hosting an Olympics builds a "village" with hotels for athletes and stadiums for the competition.

Racquets
New, hi-tech racquets send balls much faster than the old, wooden racquets could.

American Jennifer Capriati began playing tennis at the age of three when her father gave her a racquet. He soon realized just how talented his daughter was and became her coach.

Jennifer was a tennis star by the age of 15. She beat Martina Navratilova in 1991 to become the youngest-ever female semi-finalist at Wimbledon, the famous British tennis competition. A year later, she stood on a clay court in the Spanish sun looking up at the crowd.

"I'm the underdog. They're expecting me to lose," she thought. The teenager was about to play the most important match of her life – the tennis final of the 1992 Barcelona Olympic Games.

Jennifer stepped on to the court. Waiting for her on the other side was the formidable figure of Steffi Graf.

Steffi was the number two women's player in the world and the defending Olympic champion. She had not lost a set on the way to the final. Jennifer had played Steffi four times before and lost every time.

The players faced each other like ancient gladiators.

Steffi started well, hitting powerful volleys into the outer corners of the court. Jennifer stretched to return them when she could, but Steffi won the first set 6–3.

Winner
German Steffi Graf had just won the ladies' singles title at Wimbledon for the fourth time.

Feet of clay
Outdoor tennis is played on grass or on clay. The Olympic court was a clay court. Jennifer played better on clay, which has a faster surface.

33

Best shot
Steffi was amazed by Jennifer's powerful and accurate two-handed backhands.

Smashing
A smash is the most powerful tennis stroke. A player must have great confidence and concentration to hit a good smash. Steffi probably has the best smash of any female player.

Instead of giving up hope, Jennifer started the second set with increased determination and energy. If Steffi hit a forehand smash, Jennifer raced to the back of the court to return it. If Steffi fired off a forehand drive, Jennifer used her two-handed backhand to get the ball back low over the net. Jennifer won the second set 6–3.

The third and final set was finely balanced, and Steffi's play forced her young opponent to find new reserves of willpower and mental as well as physical strength.

The player leans back before she hits.

She jumps up to the ball in front of her.

She brings the racquet down hard on the ball.

Jennifer's challenge to Steffi Graf had captivated the crowd. Every point that Jennifer won was greeted by deafening cheers.

Jennifer won the next three games in a row, and the umpire finally called, "Game, set, and match to Miss Capriati!"

Jennifer's gold medal victory was one of the biggest Olympic upsets for years. Steffi had met her match in a tough teenager. Jennifer had clung to her dream of gold to become the youngest-ever Olympic tennis gold medalist.

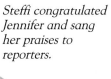

Spanish star
Jennifer had started playing tennis on a family holiday in Spain. Barcelona was therefore a fitting place for her to become a champion.

Steffi congratulated Jennifer and sang her praises to reporters.

Atlanta mascot
Atlanta's organizers had to house and feed 15,500 athletes and contend with two million visitors.

Pain and glory

"Do you think you can do it? Can America win gold?" asked the TV reporter from *Atlanta News*, thrusting a microphone at Kerri Strug. The cameras flashed.

"This is the best women's gymnastics team we've ever had," said Kerri to the crowd of over a hundred reporters gathered around her. "We're good enough to do it," she grinned.

Leaving the press behind, Kerri quickly rejoined her teammates as they set off by bus for their final training session.

There were only a few days left until the start of the 1996 Atlanta Olympics in Georgia and pressure was mounting on the team to do well. The press already had a great headline for them.

Press gangs
Press and television reporters from all the competing countries gathered for the opening ceremony.

Kerri and her six teammates were nicknamed "The Magnificent Seven." The last year had been hard work for the girls. Kerri, like the others, had been locked away with her coach, Bela Karolyi, practicing exercise after exercise. She had performed her routines on the bars, beam, floor, and vault until she knew them backward.

"In a few days," Kerri said to herself, "it will be time to show the world what we can do."

Hard work
At his gym in Houston, Texas, Bela Karolyi made Kerri train eight hours a day, six days a week.

Spectacle
President Clinton opened the 1996 Games in Atlanta. The opening ceremony was spectacular.

In team gymnastics, each team member is given a score out of 10. The best scores are added up and averaged out.

The gymnast swings and circles on the bars.

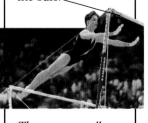

The gymnast walks, leaps, and balances on the beam.

In a vault, the gymnast runs up to the horse. Then she pushes off from it doing twists and somersaults.

The "vaulting horse" is covered with smooth leather.

Kerri and the team walked out into the Georgia Dome for the first day's competition. A roar of support rose up from the home crowd.

The gymnastics began with the bars, before moving on to the balance beam.

"We're third behind Russia and Romania," reported Bela, as Kerri stepped out to perform her floor routine. Kerri's floor moves lit up the stadium and she scored 9.825 – enough to move the U.S. team into second place.

The Americans had never beaten the Russians to an Olympic team gold medal in gymnastics. That night, Kerri wrote in her diary, "The team's all ready. Tomorrow we're going for the gold!"

On the next and final day, after more bar and floor exercises, the U.S. team was in the lead.

Only the vault – Kerri's best event – now stood between them and a gold medal.

In her floor routine, Kerri delighted the audience and the judges with her dynamic "tumbling runs" and her sense of fun.

Dominique
Dominique Moceanu was a stunning performer. She was the all-round national champion in 1995.

Perfection
In 1976, Romanian Nadia Comaneci became the first gymnast ever to score a "perfect 10." On seven occasions each judge gave her ten points.

As the event began, the first two U.S. girls achieved only average marks on the vault. At the same time, the Russians were producing their best performances so far on the floor.

Kerri watched as teammate Dominique Moceanu (mo-she-AH new) ran up for her first vault. Dominique twisted through the air gracefully. As she landed, however, she suddenly fell.

"Forget it! forget it!" ordered Bela, the coach, but everyone could see the shocked look on Dominique's face. She ran in for her second vault – and fell again. This was a disaster!

A breathless hush fell over the Dome as the crowd realized that the Russians, who were still enchanting the audience with their floor routines, were catching up.

It was now all up to Kerri.

This gymnast does a basic vaulting sequence.

Gymnast gets a good height on her takeoff

She pushes off from the bar...

...and lands cleanly.

Yurchenko
To perform a Yurchenko, the gymnast somersaults onto the vaulting horse, somersaults again, then pushes off the horse and twists.

She walked to her starting position.

She was going to perform the difficult "Yurchenko" vault.

"You know you can do it," Kerri told herself as she began her run in. Her teammates were depending on her.

Kerri somersaulted onto the horse, pushed off, and twisted beautifully in midair.

She began to open her arms for the landing position. But she had misjudged the distance to the floor mat.

Big risk
Gymnasts are
most likely to
get injured
on the vault
or the bars
because these
exercises strain
wrist and
ankle joints.

She hit the ground sooner than she expected and toppled backward! Another fall! One fall in the vault event was almost unheard of for a team – but three in a row?

As Kerri picked herself up from the floor mat, a sharp pain shot through her left foot.

"You can do it. One more. You can do it, Kerri," she heard Bela saying. She fought back the tears.

As Kerri limped back to the run-up area, she knew her ankle was badly injured. She knew she should withdraw from the competition. But she also knew that her team needed her second vault.

Kerri ran in again, terrified of falling in front of the billion people watching in the stadium and on TV. This time she twisted through the air and landed cleanly. She went into the finishing position, but a second later collapsed in agony.

Despite her terrible pain, Kerri had scored 9.712 – enough for the U.S. team to keep the lead.

"You did it!" beamed Bela. He carried her in his arms to the medal ceremony and held her as she collected her gold medal and the crowd cheered on.

End of an era
The Atlanta Olympics, the last of the 20th century, ended as spectacularly as it had begun.

Opening ceremony:
Friday,
September 15,
2000

Closing ceremony:
Sunday,
October 1,
2000

Sydney 2000

The year 2000 Olympics will be the most spectacular ever. They will be held in Sydney, Australia, and involve more than 10,000 athletes from 200 countries around the globe, as well as 5,000,000 spectators.

New sports will include taekwondo (tie-kwon-DOE) and the triathlon.

More than 3.5 billion people are expected to watch the Games on TV.

Different sports

 Aquatics

Archery

Athletics

 Badminton

Baseball

Basketball

 Boxing

Canoe/kayak

Cycling

 Equestrian

Fencing

Football

 Gymnastics

Handball

Hockey

 Judo

Pentathlon

Rowing

 Sailing

Shooting

Softball

 Table tennis

Taekwondo

Tennis

Triathlon

Volleyball

Weightlifting

Wrestling

Sydney celebrates
When Australia won its bid to host the Olympic Games in 2000 the Australians were overjoyed. Sydney Harbor was alight with dazzling celebrations that lasted for days.

Officials:
Total number of Olympic officials: 5,100

Village
This will have 477 houses and more than 330 units to house 15,300 people.

Money
Cost of hosting the Games: A$2.6 billion

Olympic record breakers

Most medals

Most gold medals
10 Raymond Ewry (YOU-ree) (USA)
Standing, high, long, and triple
jumps, 1900, 1904, 1906, 1908

Most medals in total (female)
18 Larisa Latynina (la-tee-NEE-na)
(USSR – gymnastics) 1956–64

Most medals in total (male)
15 Nikolay (NIK-oh-lie) Adrianov
(USSR – gymnastics) 1972–1980

Most gold medals won in one Games
7 Mark Spitz (USA – swimming,
including three medals for relays) 1972

Most medals by nation

1	United States	2,015
2	Soviet Union	1,234
3	Great Britain	635
4	France	562
5	Germany*	516
6	Sweden	459
7	Italy	444
8	Hungary	425
9	East Germany*	410
10	Australia	294

*Germany split into West
Germany and East Germany
between 1968 and 1988.*

Track Olympic and world records

100 meters: 9.84 seconds – Donovan Bailey (Canada), Atlanta 1996

200 meters: 19.32 seconds – Michael Johnson (USA), Atlanta 1996

400 meters: 43.86 seconds – Lee Evans (USA), Mexico City 1968

1,500 meters: 3 minutes 35.6 seconds – Herb Elliot (Australia),
Rome 1960

10,000 meters: 27 minutes 38.4 seconds – Lasse Viren (Finland),
Montreal 1976

The fastest woman ever was Florence Griffith-Joyner (USA),
who ran at 24.58 miles per hour (39.56 kilometers per hour)
in the women's 100-meters final in Seoul, South Korea, 1988.

Youngest and oldest

Youngest competitor
7-10 years old:
unknown French boy
used by the Dutch rowing
team in 1900

Youngest gold medalist
13 years old:
Marjorie Gestring
(USA – diving) 1936

Oldest competitor
72 years old: Oscar Swahn
(Sweden – shooting) 1920

Oldest female competitor
70 years old: Lorna
Johnstone (Great Britain –
equestrian) 1972

Oldest gold medalist
60 years old: Oscar Swahn
(Sweden – shooting) 1908

Fun Olympic facts

• Mongolia is the nation whose athletes have won most medals (13) but never a gold!

• Roswitha Krause (KROW-se) (GDR) is the only woman to have won medals in two sports:
1968 – swimming
1976–80 – athletics

• Daniel Carroll won rugby gold medals for two countries:
1908 Australia, 1920 USA

• In 1992, Russian gymnast Vitaly Scherbo (SHER-bow) won four gold medals in a single day.

• In 1988, Byun Jong II (BEE-yun YONG) of South Korea staged the longest protest about a judge's decision. He remained in the boxing ring for one hour and seven minutes, even after the lights had been switched off.

• Only three countries have competed in every Olympic Games – Australia, France, and Greece.

• The most competitors at a summer games is 10,744 (7,060 men, 3,684 women) at Atlanta, USA, 1996.

Glossary

Archeologist
Someone who studies ancient times and peoples by examining what is left of their buildings, tools, weapons, art, etc.

Ceremony
A set of acts done in a particular way to celebrate a special occasion.

Coach
A person who teaches and trains students, athletes, and performers.

Competitor
A person who competes for a prize.

Discipline
A particular event for which an athlete has been trained.

Disqualify
To take an athlete out of a competition because he or she has broken a rule.

Foul
An act that breaks the rules of a game or athletic event.

Gladiator
A man of ancient Rome who used to fight men or animals to entertain people.

Host
A person or people who provides guests with places of comfort and entertainment in their home or city.

Mascot
A person, animal, or thing that is supposed to bring good luck by being present.

Motto
A brief saying that is used as a rule to live by or a rule to encourage true sportsmanship.

Olympian
A man or woman who competes in the Olympic Games.

Opponent
A person who opposes or is against another in a fight or contest.

Qualify
To make fit or be fit for specific work or a particular activity.

Rival
A person who tries to do something better than another.

Rostrum
A raised platform on a stage where a speaker or a prizewinner stands.

Routine
A series of steps for a dance or gymnastic performance; a regular way of doing something, fixed by rules or habit.

Spectator
A person who watches something without taking part.

Sprint
To run at full speed.

Stadium
A place that is used for outdoor athletic events and other activities.

Tactic
A skilful method used by people to help them succeed in a task or a game.

Tribute
Something that is given, done, or said to show thanks or respect.

Umpire
A person who ensures that a game is played fairly and by the rules.

Underdog
A person, team, or side that is expected to lose a contest of some kind.

Willpower
A strength of will, mind, or purpose.